Gateway to Heaven

Lillian C. Parkin

What a scene!
Beauty like gates to Paradise;
The swirling mists
Began to rise;
The sun broke through
With rays of gold
And touched the autumn
Leaves, grown old
Through summer's growth;
Blessed the lake
With solemn oath—
A path of gold from side to side
Across the water dark and wide.
The mist took on the shining sheen;
Behind it's shifting shapes were seen
The stately mountain

All newly dressed
To greet the frosty winter
In her best—
A blue smoke gown overlayed
With mantilla of the frailest lace,
And hood to frame her lovely face
Woven from lightest flakes of snow
And trimmed by sun's pale golden glow.
Her hair was twined
With brightest garland
Of autumn leaves all red and scarlet,
Orange, tan, the touch of gold;
No mortal's brush created this—
The merest glimpse
Of Heaven's bliss.

Photo Opposite
REFLECTIONS OF AUTUM
Highland, Maine
Dick Dietrich, Photographe

Who Dares Call November Dull?

Irene Lucido

Who dares call November dull?
Why, look, she is a carnival
Of whirling colors, gay parades,
Leaves in uniform, flower maids
Of harvest sing.
Birds still here, and on the wing,
Goblins stir the pools of night,
Moon and stars are silver bright;
Who dares call November dull—
When she's flash and flame—
And wonderful!

Photo Opposite
KANCAMANGUS HIGHWAY
White Mountains, New Hampshire
Larry Lefever/Grant Heilman Photography, Inc.

Autumn

The sun rose slowly above the horizon,
Frost covered the grass like a blanket,
The clouds were lined with gold,
    giving the sky a majestic look.
Birds opened their wings,
    and took flight southward,
The leaves glistened with the morning dew,
And the autumn wind howled,
As the world blossomed in color.

Michael Bostian
Fairfax, Virginia

Indiana Autumn

Oh, beautiful
    autumn leaves
Floating, drifting
    to the ground,
Vivid colors of
    red and gold
Against the
    Indiana countryside,

Indian corn of
    many colors,
Wee pumpkins and
    tiny gourds
Announce the arrival
    of fall.

Leaves of autumn,
    red and yellow,
Early morning fog
    and dewy grass,
Cold brisk mornings,
    warm afternoons—
Winter is on
    the way.

Dolores McQueary
Terre Haute, Indiana

Reflections

The Autumn Time of Year

I love the autumn time of year
When winds will howl or sigh;
It seems as though they're echoing
Sweet summer's sad good-bye.
"Farewell, farewell," they call to me,
"Soon winter will be here,
So I bring you a special gift
To fill your world with cheer:
A treasure chest of emeralds,
Of rubies, and of gold;
I'll swirl my jewels across the land
In colors bright and bold.
Then when the world is cold and white
Viewed from your windowpane,
You will recall the glow of fall
To warm your heart again."

Sandra Town Lytle
Moscow, Indiana

9

American Autumn

Gail Brook Burket

Now colors glow like flames of apple wood,
Not faery green of April nor the dull
Gray monochrome of winter long withstood,
But jewel-hued and boldly beautiful.
The crimson oaks and scarlet maples seem
Like hallelujahs rising to the sky.
The trumpet notes of golden poplars gleam
And yellow banners of witch hazel fly.

The sun soon leaves the cupola of blue
And shadows flock like swallows after flight
Into the meadows where clear drops of dew
Begin to glimmer in the fading light.
And from the shoulders of the hills there fall
The mellow ripples of a paisley shawl.

Indian Summer

Helen Harrington

Frost, in a brief apology
For all it had to do
To every bush and plant and tree
Gives us a scenic view,

Sets the autumn woods on fire!
Paints the gardens bright:
Gilds the weed patch and the briar
With sudden golden light.

War bonnet beauty stomps the fields
As ruddy leaves outrun
The morning chill and Jack Frost yields
To Indian summer sun.

Beauty

Alice B. Dorland

Beauty is in the eyes
Of him who sees its loveliness.

And so is God;
And so is Heaven.

Teach us to see
Beauty in each familiar sight,

In rain, in winter's gray,
In darkest night,

As well as
In the day's clear light.

For beauty is in the heart
Of him who knows its loveliness.

Photo Opposite
OLD MILL
Jericho, Vermont
enry J. Hupp/Laatsch-Hupp Photo

THANKSGIVING SEASON

Gloria Ingram Roberts

The season pours its gifts in lavish measure:
Soil, seed, and rain, sunshine through summer days,
Autumn leaves, windsong, the harvest treasure—
So we pour out our muted songs of praise.
Gourds, nuts and fruits are stored in abundance
On cellar shelves where mingled odors cloy;
The autumn wind wafts the subtle fragrance
Of wide-flung harvest fields which we enjoy.
Now garnered in from rows of shining sheaves
Corn is heaped high as fretted bins will hold;
Just so, little gracious thoughts that leave
Hearts worshipful swell a gratitude untold.
From the bounty of goodness, our needs are filled;
And from hearts overflowing is gratitude spilled.

HARVEST TIME
Dick Dietrich, Photograp

FROM MY
G·A·R·D·E·N
JOURNAL

Deana Deck

Squash and Pumpkins

In art and life, on magazine covers or as holiday table decor, Thanksgiving cornucopias usually include a variety of squashes and small pumpkins, in addition to the other symbols of a bountiful harvest. It's not surprising that such an all-American holiday would feature such all-American vegetables.

When the Pilgrims and the Indians sat down together at the first Thanksgiving meal, the table was loaded with native food, much of which was previously unknown to the Europeans. There were grapes, persimmons, and pecans; turkey, deer, rabbit, and squirrel; sweet potatoes, corn, beans, squash, and pumpkin.

Squash and pumpkin are members of the *Cucurbita pepo* family, which includes cucumbers, watermelons, cantaloupes, luffas and gourds. Many of the most familiar varieties of summer squash and pumpkin originated in Mexico and Central America. Winter squashes originated in the Andes region of Argentina.

Because there had been constant traffic and trading between North and South America for hundreds of years, Native Americans were enjoying squash and pumpkin as a regular part of their diets long before the arrival of the Pilgrims. Winter squash was particularly valued because it was so easily stored for use in the long, cold New England winters.

While somewhat different in taste and appearance, squash and pumpkin share many characteristics. Among them is the need for a vast amount of growing space. Many of the popular varieties produce vines up to ten feet long. To save space, the growing tips of these vines can be pruned back, but only after the fruit has set. When pruning, it is important to leave plenty of leaves on the vine to nourish the fruit.

Because of their need for space, pumpkin and winter squash rows should be planted at least six to ten feet apart. For gardeners with a limited area to cultivate, however, there is good news. A number of "compact" strains of squash have been developed which do not grow long vines, and both squash and pumpkins can be grown successfully on trellises. (Heavy pumpkins and large squash should be provided with extra support to hold them firmly against the trellis. Old pantyhose are quite handy for this purpose.)

Another option is to stick to bush-type squash varieties like zucchini and crookneck, which can be planted in rows only three to four feet apart. These can even be grown in containers.

Squash, pumpkin, and their cousins are all warm season vegetables. Young plants are very vulnerable to frost, and seeds require warm soil to germinate. In temperate zones and farther south, they can be planted in late April or early

May. Plan on two winter squash plants per person and two summer squash plants per four to six people.

Northern gardeners can get a head start on their local growing season by starting seeds indoors in individual peat pots. They can then be transplanted in April, pot and all, without disturbing tender roots. Individual plants can be protected with hot caps and entire rows can be covered with plastic or spun polypropylene. The plastic can be easily draped over bended wire to form protective tunnels and the lightweight polypropylene can be "floated" directly on the young plants. Either will provide several degrees of added warmth to protect against late freezes.

Raise the plastic covers for two hours each morning to insure pollination. I find that keeping the young plants completely covered as much as possible helps avoid problems with the squash vine borer by preventing the moth from laying her eggs on the plant.

For the absolute best harvest, plant on raised hills of soil enriched with compost. This provides the roots with several inches of well-tilled, rich soil in which to grow. When the plants begin to blossom, side-dress them by placing about one tablespoon of 5-10-10 fertilizer in a shallow trench around each plant—about three or four inches away from the stem. Cover this fertilizer well with soil. If the plant's leaves contact the fertilizer they will be burned.

There are literally hundreds of varieties of squash and pumpkin from which to choose. My advice is to peruse the garden catalogs and find those varieties that sound the tastiest and that best suit your needs and growing conditions.

If you want to store food for winter, then be sure to plant several winter varieties as well as tender summer squash. Winter squash choices include acorn, butternut, hubbard, and the unusual "spaghetti" squash.

If you wish to provide children with pumpkins for carving Jack-o'-Lanterns at Halloween, select a Big Max, Big Moon, or other large variety, but if sweet pumpkin pies are your goal, try the classic Small Sugar, also known as the New England pie pumpkin.

If you enjoy pumpkin seeds, choose a variety that forms no hulls around the seeds, such as the Lady Godiva or the Hungarian Mammoth.

Summer squash matures much earlier than winter squash. You can begin harvesting zucchini within forty-eight to fifty days. Cut summer squash from the vine when it is young and tender. Zucchini should be about eight inches long, crooknecks one to two inches in diameter, and bush scallops three to four inches across.

Most winter squash and pumpkins take about 110 days to mature, and should not be harvested until fully ripe. In fact, some cold weather adds to the flavor, by increasing sugar content. The squash is ripe when the skin has hardened and changed color. Green varieties like acorn squash will pick up some orange or yellow tints and butternut squash will turn completely tan.

Leave a one-inch stem on each fruit and cure winter squash in a warm, dry, ventilated spot for about two weeks before storing. To help protect them, dip each squash into solution of nine parts water to one part chlorine bleach, then air dry. Store them where the temperature will remain in the 50 to 60° range, and do not allow the fruit to touch. Stuffing wadded up newspaper between squashes is helpful. They can be stored from four to six months. If mildew appears on the skin of your winter squash, remove it by wiping the squash with a cloth dipped in vegetable oil.

There are an abundance of ways to serve all varieties of squash, but the prolific zucchini seems to have inspired the greatest number of recipes. My own method of using the inevitable excess of zucchini is to slice them and blanch them in the microwave, puree them in a blender, and put them into heat-sealable freezer bags. I store them in the freezer until time to make up a batch of vegetable soup, and use the pureed zucchini as a soup base. It's a delicious, nutritious, and very practical solution to what sometimes turns out to be an overwhelmingly bountiful harvest.

Squash and pumpkins, growing in abundance all across America for as long as we have been a nation, are the perfect symbol for the Thanksgiving season—a celebration both of Nature's bounty and of our unique national heritage.

Deana Deck lives in Nashville, Tennessee, where her garden column is a regular feature in the Tennessean.

PUMPKINS AND GOUR[]
Libba Gillum, Photograp[]

THIS PRAYER I MAKE

William Wordsworth

This prayer I make,
Knowing that nature never did betray
The heart that loved her; 'tis her privilege,
Through all the years of this our life, to lead
From joy to joy; for she can so inform

The mind that is within us, so impress
With quietness and beauty, and so feed
With lofty thoughts, that neither evil tongues,
Rash judgments, nor the sneers of selfish men,
Nor greetings where no kindness is, nor all
The dreary intercourse of daily life,
Shall e'er prevail against us, or disturb
Our cheerful faith, that all which we behold
Is full of blessings.

SYMBOLS OF THANKSGIVING

Mary O'Conner

The sun may trace the beauty of a fern
Upon a golden pumpkin or a stone
Just as our nation's flag may rise alone
In majesty where eagles glide and turn.

The stripes are red as blood in veins that burn
With gratitude and warmth: our very own
Inheritance of Pilgrim flesh and bone,
Symbolic of our past, from which we learn.

The oak tree scatters bronze upon the stream
Like moulting plumage at the season's height;
Man feels the tang of thanks that tempers his goal
And makes him humble, glad to share the dream:
The symbols God designed, till faith and right
Enshrine Thanksgiving's meaning in the soul.

Not Ours Alone

Marie Hunter Dawson

We have upon our table here a loaf of bread.
The cream-white slices golden-rimmed
Down to the fragrant crust are passed around—
And passed around again. Then, when the loaf is used,
Another takes its place upon our plate!

There is a pitcher on our table, too, full to the brim of milk—
Rich, white, foaming. I pour till everyone has had a share,
As each drinks his cup I say—not hesitating—
"Have some more, please do!" For we have milk for all
And some to spare.

We have a lamp here, too, which gives us needed light
By day or night. There is no darkened room,
No sunless days, no long black nights,
Because we have a lamp
And with its light we have no fear upon our way.

And yet our loaf is not for us alone.
But, sharing, we may pass our bread out yonder
Where a waiting throng with searching arms outstretched
And faces pinched, yet smiling, may lift life-giving portions
From our family plate.

The contents of our pitcher, too, we share,
Filling their cups long empty, bringing new life
To thin parched lips long since resigned
To hopeless craving! Ah, yes, our lamps we share.
Not for the confines of our home alone,
Its light must serve a larger sphere. We place it high
Upon God's sill of love and let its rays go out
Farther and farther until the last faint rays
Become transfused in endless light.

Sustenance and light!
Not ours alone these priceless things to have,
For only as we share our bread and milk
Are we sustained in growth.
Only as we lift our lamp a little higher
Can it shine for us and them upon the holy way.
Sustenance! Light! God, may we worthy be
To eat, to drink, to walk in Light with Thee!

Photo Opposite
DINING ROOM WITH PINE ANTIQUE
Julie Mikos/Jessie Walker Associates

A SLICE OF LIFE

— Edgar A. Guest —

Thanksgiving

Thankful for the glory of the old Red, White, and Blue,
For the spirit of America that still is staunch and true,
For the laughter of our children and the sunlight
    in their eyes,
And the joy of radiant mothers and their
    evening lullabies;
And thankful that our harvests wear no taint of
    blood today,
But were sown and reaped by toilers who were light
    of heart and gay.

Thankful for the riches that are ours to claim and ke
The joy of honest labor and the boon of happy slee
For each little family circle where there is no
    empty chair
Save where God has sent the sorrow for the loving
    hearts to bear;
And thankful for the loyal souls and brave hearts
    of the past
Who builded that contentment should be with us
    to the last.

thankful for the plenty that our peaceful land
     has blessed,
or the rising sun that beckons every man to
     do his best,
or the goal that lies before him and the promise
     when he sows
hat his hand shall reap the harvest, undisturbed by
     cruel foes;
or the flaming torch of justice, symbolizing
     as it burns:
here none may rob the toiler of the prize he
     fairly earns.

Today our thanks we're giving for the riches
     that are ours,
For the red fruits of the orchards and the perfume
     of the flowers,
For our homes with laughter ringing and our
     hearthfires blazing bright,
For our land of peace and plenty and our land of
     truth and right;
And we're thankful for the glory of the old
     Red, White, and Blue,
For the spirit of our fathers and a manhood that
     is true.

Edgar A. Guest began his illustrious career in 1895 at the age of fourteen when his work first appeared in the Detroit Free Press. *His column was syndicated in over 300 newspapers, and he became known as "The Poet of the People."*

27

Thanksgiving

Estelle S. Rizk

Not while a dogwood
   blooms on the hill,
And a redbird calls
   with a gay, glad trill;
Not while a fire glows
   in my hearth,
And my rooms are happy
   with childish mirth,
Not while winds moan
   through a sycamore—
Will I say I have nothing
   to give thanks for!

Not while I have
   a flower to bloom,
And a cheery lamp
   to light my room;
Not while a friend
   drops in to call
And trees blaze scarlet
   in the fall,
While I've tasks to be done
   as best I can,
And I've a spark of faith
   in my fellow man—
Not while grey fog
   covers the moor
Will I say I have nothing
   to give thanks for.

CHRONICLE

Lansing Christman

A touch of summer smiled through the midst of autumn one Thanksgiving as my father and I drew in hay from a stack we had built in July. The stack was in the meadow on the flat across the road from the barns, built on a gentle slope of outcropping rock and shale.

It had been a good year for timothy, and the barns were full at harvest's end, with no room for the crop from one meadow. To preserve this hay, we put it into a stack, packed layer by layer, with each forkful slightly overlapping the other, much as bricks overlap in a wall.

By late November, the barns had room for our hay stack. As we removed it, forkful by forkful, for hauling to the barn, we discovered beneath it an array of summer blooms, colorful and dried and well-preserved, as though a lover of flowers had pressed them in a book.

30

I was thankful then that we had never been too concerned when Queen Anne's lace, daisies, primrose, yarrow, and St. John's wort flourished in the fields, displaying their blooms in the midst of the ripening hay. It may not have been a mark of good husbandry, but I cherished the beauty of those blossoming "weeds," just as I have always cherished our garden flowers.

This Thanksgiving bouquet is one I have kept in my heart and treasured in my memories. I could picture myself again at work in the heat of summer, listening to the song of the field sparrow in the pasture beyond the brook, or the whistle of the lark in the meadow, or the chattering of the swallows sweeping and diving about the barns.

I read a message in that November floral bouquet, a reminder to nurture and safeguard the natural environment around us. That was more than sixty years ago, and I am thankful in these later years of life that I have been among those who have followed a basic commandment to be "caretakers of the earth."

The author of two published books, Lansing Christman has been contributing to Ideals *for almost twenty years. Mr. Christman has also been published in several American, foreign, and braille anthologies. He lives in rural South Carolina.*

CRAFTWORKS

Thanksgiving Dinner Placemats and Napkins

Marty Brooks

Many early settlers decorated their homes with beautiful stenciling. Make this Thanksgiving special with stenciled placemats and napkins you've painted yourself.

Materials Needed:

Purchased placemats and napkins
  (cotton-polyester blends work best)
Masking tape
Plastic stencils in "Welcome Friends" and "Little
  Wooden House" patterns, or similar patterns
Fabric Paint: Harvest Gold, Homestead Brown,
  Shamrock Green, Country Red
Saucer
3/8 to 5/8-inch Round Stencil Brush
Paper towels
Disappearing marker (available at craft supply
  stores)

Directions:

1. Wash placemats and napkins with any laundry detergent which does not contain fabric softener. Dry without dryer sheets. Iron if necessary.

2. Position the stencil on the fabric and draw around the openings with the disappearing marker. This will help position the stencil correctly for each color.

3. Tape over the stencil holes which are *not* to be in the first color.

4. Working on a flat, hard surface protected with plastic, place the stencil on the fabric, matching the marker lines to the stencil openings. Tape the sides of the stencil to the fabric.

5. Pour a little of the first color into a saucer. Dip the brush into the paint then daub it onto dry paper towels to remove all excess paint. Gently bounce the brush on the stencil areas you are painting with the first color. *Do not use a sweeping motion as this will force paint under the stencil.* To add more paint layers, repeat as before, always daubing the brush onto dry paper towels to remove all of the excess paint.

6. When all of the open parts of the stencil are painted with the first color, carefully remove the tape and lift the stencil from the fabric. Rinse the stencil and brush and dry completely.

7. Before painting in the second color, tape over all the openings on the stencil which are *not* for the second color.

8. When the first color is dry to the touch, tape the stencil to the fabric being careful to match the previously drawn lines and proceed as with the first color.

9. Repeat this process until the design is complete. Repeat stenciling for each placemat needed. Stencil napkins as above, using only a portion of the total design and positioning design to show in corner of napkin after folding. Stencil napkin flat, not folded so that color does not "bleed through" the fabric.

10. Allow paint to dry overnight. Heat-set by either tossing in a dryer on high for 10 minutes, or cover the design with a pressing cloth and hold a warm iron over design for 10 seconds.

Harbinger of Winter

I'm bid forty; who'll make it forty-five. Now who'll make it fifty. Now sixty. Fifty-five. Now sixty. Who'll give me sixty? Come on boys, a pretty girl made this pie, and she's a good cook, too—just like her ma."

"Sixty," someone yells from the back of the room.

"Sixty, now make it seventy-five," the auctioneer chants as he starts off the first pie supper held in Missouri this fall.

Pie suppers may be a remnant of the era of the button shoe, the horse and buggy, and the kerosene lamp, but they still rate as one of the most popular community entertainments in the Middle West.

Practically every little country school in that section of the United States becomes the scene of one pie supper during each school term.

The pie supper season starts in September, gains momentum through October, and rolls to a stop in early November. In fact, Middle Westerners don't have to wait for the leaves on the sugar maple to turn red before they realize fall is coming; the pie supper at the little one room school house is an earlier and surer sign.

Everybody in the community goes to the pie supper, whether he has children in school or not. And each girl—big and little, old and young—brings a pie. Row after row of pies, topped with fluffy white meringue or spread across with neat little pastry strips, proudly sit on the table.

As each pie arrives, a number is placed on it, and that number recorded in a book. Theoretically, the number is secret—but that is theory only. For if a boy wants to know the number of a certain girl's pie, the person keeping the books willingly lets him look it up. It's really good business, for if a boy knows the number of the pie he wants, he will bid more for it. Sometimes, of course, jokesters switch the numbers on him, and he discovers he paid a big price for the wrong pie.

Before the auctioning of pies begins, the pupils of the school entertain the audience with songs, dialogues, short plays, or recitations.

Then the auctioneer selected by the teacher comes to the front of the room and takes over. The auctioneer is always one of the best-liked men in the community and invariably deep laugh-wrinkles play around his eyes.

Before the auctioneer actually starts selling the pies, there are a few other money-making schemes he must promote for the benefit of the school.

First he auctions off a cake one of the women in the neighborhood has baked and donated to the school. Then a quart of jelly beans is brought out, and everyone guesses the number of beans in the jar—at one cent a guess. The person coming closest to the correct number wins the prize.

Then a box of candy is put up as a prize to the most popular or the most beautiful girl, and the boys vote—for one cent a vote. A boy who thinks his girl must be named "the most popular young lady present here tonight" has to dig deep into his hip pocket.

These prizes cause much laughter and teasing. They also draw in money, for votes are sold at a penny each for every event.

A pie may sell for any amount from a dime to ten dollars, depending upon its attractiveness and the culinary ability or popularity of the girl who brought it.

If a boy has his heart set on buying a certain girl's pie, the other boys often run up the price. However, the bidders always take a risk, for sometimes the joke boomerangs and the pie is dropped to one of them for a high sum.

These pie suppers serve a double purpose: they make money for the school and also provide and excuse for a community gathering. The average pie supper clears from $15 to $50, although occasionally the sum runs up to $90. This money buys something the school needs—a new map, books for the school library, or a new ball and bat.

Although the money they bring in is useful, pie suppers really stand out for the community spirit they arouse. In many rural communities the pie supper highlights the social events of the year. Everyone goes, and everyone has fun.

Originally printed in *The Christian Science Monitor Magazine*, November 8, 1941.

Key to Joy

Lucille V. McCurtain

I know no key to joy like thankfulness;
It opens every bar across my way.
Just to feel thankful lifts my heart to God;
To wake and say, "Thanks, God, for everything:
For this sweet breath I draw, for those I love;
For peace within in spite of strife without;
For this good life which gives a chance each day
To be of use to someone in this world."
So thankfulness has opened up my door
And all the tenseness, fear of the unknown,
Drops from my limbs and leaves me free to live.
A grateful heart is cleansed of selfishness,
Is fragrant and receptive to God's love.
Each hour His bounty fills and overflows
My every need, and grants the power to share.
For daily there is excess to be given;
And sharing I can know how glad God is
To give to me out of His infinite store,
To hear just one soul say, "Thanks be to God!"

Photo Opposite
ANTIQUE THANKSGIVING CAR
Ina Mackey, Photographer

Pocahontas

Ever since John Smith first told the story of his capture and imprisonment by the great chief Powhatan and his subsequent salvation by the chief's young daughter, the legend of Pocahontas has been a part of American folklore. An endless succession of poets and storytellers have told and retold the tale of this young Indian girl, so smitten by the dashing English captain that she risked her own life to gain his release.

Unfortunately, as with most legends, the story of Pocahontas, as we have come to know it, is more romantic fiction than historical fact. Pocahontas was not simply a young, innocent girl who acted bravely out of love; she was a courageous and compassionate woman who, in her lifetime, brought together two cultures destined to be at odds.

Pocahontas was the daughter of Powhatan, the great and powerful chief of the Indians of seventeenth century tidewater Virginia. She likely would have had an ordinary childhood, had she not been born on the verge of a great upheaval in the life of her people. In 1607 when Pocahontas was only twelve or thirteen years old, Powhatan society was permanently altered by the landing of three English ships in Chesapeake Bay. The ships carried colonists eager to claim a portion of the New World in the name of the British crown. Unfortunately, they sought to claim the very portion of that world that belonged to Powhatan and his people.

The landing of these strange men so close to his home troubled Chief Powhatan. While he was fearful, however, he was also cautious. Powhatan did not attack the colonists; but when English Captain John Smith and his explorers ventured too close to the chief's settlement, they were captured and held prisoner.

Chief Powhatan was not a cruel man; neither was he naive. He knew that Smith and his followers were a threat to the peaceful existence of his people. The chief kept Smith prisoner for several weeks, probably in hopes of discovering as much as possible about the settlers. Only after he was convinced of a serious threat did Powhatan plan Smith's execution.

But that execution never took place—Pocahontas would not allow it. Youth and inexperience freed her from her father's fears; to the chief's daughter, Smith was less a threat than a novelty. When the time came for his execution, Pocahontas pleaded for John Smith's life. Her pleas were so successful that the chief not only spared Smith's life, but transported him safely back to the Jamestown settlement.

Pocahontas had made a powerful impression on Smith, who returned her kindness by making her a welcome friend in his colony. In the winter that followed Smith's capture, Pocahontas visited Jamestown often, bringing food and supplies and advice without which the colony may not have made it through a season full of disease and famine. At Pocahontas' urging, Smith released several Indian prisoners his colony had been holding; not long after, Pocahontas convinced her father to invite Smith and a small group of settlers to their village, this time as welcome guests.

Eventually, the colonists overthrew John Smith and sent him back to England. In the years following his departure, little was recorded of Pocahontas and her dealings with the settlers. We can assume, however, that she did not lose touch; in the spring of 1614, she married colonist John Rolfe. The couple settled on a tract of land granted them by chief Powhatan, and their marriage began a period of great harmony between the colonists and the Indians.

As Mrs. John Rolfe, Pocahontas became a member of colonial society. She embraced Christianity and was baptized Rebecca; and she gave birth to one son, who was raised a British citizen. With Rolfe, Pocahontas visited England, where she was presented to King James I in 1617. Pocahontas died while in England and is buried at the parish church of St. George in Gravesend.

The good relations between her people and the English settlers that Pocahontas helped foster in her own lifetime did not last. Neither did the Powhatan people. Today, all that most Americans know of the Powhatans is the legend of Pocahontas. In her own day Indians and settlers alike often saw Pocahontas as a naive young woman so entranced by the wonders of English society that she gave up her own culture; but today many see her as an innocent girl whose kindness was taken advantage of by settlers anxious to settle Virginia.

Neither tells the whole story. Pocahontas gave up much of her native culture for John Smith and her husband John Rolfe. At the same time, however, her familiarity in the Jamestown colony rendered Indian culture much less strange and frightening to the British settlers. The true legacy of Pocahontas is not the story of a love between a young Indian girl and a handsome English captain, but of a woman with an open heart and an open mind who lived by the rules of kindness and charity, not race and nationality.

POPCORN TOPPINGS

Popcorn is a natural for Thanksgiving. It is also a natural for those keeping a watch on fat and cholesterol. These delicious popcorn toppings add variety to an all-American snack without adding calories. For all toppings, begin with one tablespoon of popcorn popped in a hot air popper or in a heavy skillet over high heat. Do not add oil. Once popped, toss the popcorn with one of these delicious toppings.

Fiesta Butter Popcorn

(63 calories per serving)

1   teaspoon butter or margarine, melted
1/8 teaspoon chili powder
1   dash garlic salt
1   dash paprika

Combine all ingredients. Toss with warm popcorn until coated.

Parmesan Popcorn

(73 calories per serving)

1 1/2   teaspoons grated Parmesan cheese
1   teaspoon butter or margarine, melted

Combine cheese and butter or margarine. T with warm popcorn until coated.

Lemon-Basil Popcorn

(63 calories per serving)

1   teaspoon butter or margarine, melted
1/2 teaspoon basil, crushed
3-4 drops fresh lemon juice

Combine all ingredients. Toss with warm popcorn until coated.

Green and Gold Buttered Popcorn

(63 calories per serving)

1   teaspoon butter or margarine, melted
1   teaspoon snipped parsley
1/2 teaspoon finely chopped chives

Toss warm popcorn with butter or margarine Sprinkle with parsley and chives. Salt to taste.

First Thanksgiving

Jessie Wilmore Murton

The bleak wind writhes and whistles, as it spits
White flakes against the corncrib's bulging slits
And sifts them underneath the cabin door.
But firelight leaps and flickers on the floor
Inside, from the wide chimney place. Its gleams

Fall on a spinning wheel; and rosy beams
Glint the two candlesticks of quaint old brass,
The copper kettle, and an old-world glass.

A rude log cabin, in a hostile land;
The frugal fare, upon the rough-hewn board;
Crude furnishings, wrought patiently by hand;
And homespun garments! Yet for this small hoard,
Our brave forefathers still could gladly raise
Their grateful songs of thankfulness, and praise.

Jamestown, Virginia

Thirteen years before the Pilgrims set foot on Plymouth Rock, English settlers disembarked from three ships onto what is now Virginia soil to establish the first permanent English settlement in the New World. Like the Pilgrims, and the other Puritan settlers of the Massachusetts Bay Colony, these hardy souls made a treacherous journey across the Atlantic, departing from London on December 20, 1606, and finally spying land on April 26, 1607. They, too, left behind the comforts of home and family to face an uncertain future in a wild and inhospitable land. But unlike their fellow citizens who would settle to the north, the 1607 party were not running away from persecution or corruption.

The purpose of this venture into an unknown land was not freedom from England, but profit. The settlers had come to make fortunes for themselves and the crown.

On April 29, the settlers erected a wooden cross on the sand dunes and gave thanks for their safe journey. The next day, the three ships entered the fertile waters of Chesapeake Bay and landed across Hampton Roads at what is now Point Comfort. For the next two weeks, the settlers explored along the banks of the James River, below and above the present site of Jamestown. They named the site they chose in honor of their king, James I, who had sanctioned this journey of mercantile-minded settlers.

Once the site had been determined, all 104 of the weary travelers disembarked from the ships, *Susan Constant*, *Godspeed*, and *Discovery*. The date was May 13, 1607. By the end of June, the settlement was well-established, with a government appointed by the king, houses for all, and good relations with the local Indians, the Powhatans.

During the summer months, however, the Indians turned hostile; provisions ran low as the food spoiled and the brackish drinking water proved hazardous. The resulting disease epidemics killed daily. Conditions were so bad that the settlers threw out the presiding leader of the governing council and then turned out his replacement. The third governor was Captain John Smith. Smith was a capable and disciplined leader; but by the time he took over as governor, the settlers numbered fewer than fifty. During the next years, only his tough, dictatorial leadership and his policy of "no work, no food" kept the colony intact.

In January of 1608 more ships arrived, bringing new supplies. Soon after, however, disaster struck again when the fort caught fire and many of the houses and provisions were lost. During the months of rebuilding the settlers would not have survived without the help of the Powhatans, especially the corn the Indians provided for them. This friendly relationship between settlers and Indians came about through the efforts of Smith and Pocahontas, daughter of Chief Powhatan.

In October, 1608, a ship arrived carrying workmen sent by the crown to produce glass and wood products. The ship also carried the first two women settlers to Jamestown. But just as the settlement began to gain strength and stability, bad luck returned, this time in the form of a supply ship loaded with four hundred inexperienced settlers, wet and moldy provisions, fever, plague, and a growing population of rats. The rats ate almost all of the stored corn, and the winter of 1609 became known as "The Starving Time." Settlers died from malnutrition, exposure, and disease, and the population shrank from five hundred to fifty-nine.

And the profit-making ventures? Over the years the colony experimented with several crops, but only the tobacco proved profitable. King James I regarded it as "lothsome to the eye, hatefull to the nose, harmful to the braine, and dangerous to the lungs," but his subjects disagreed. In 1619, 40,000 pounds were shipped from Virginia to England, and tobacco became the basis for Jamestown's survival. The colony became the capital city of Virginia and the scene of the meeting of the Virginia House of Burgesses in 1619, the first representative assembly in the New World. In 1698 a fire destroyed the State House and the government moved to Middle Plantation, which was renamed Williamsburg. Jamestown fell into disuse and decay.

Today, foundations of houses and public buildings, remains of streets, a variety of artifacts,

and the Old Church Tower are all that exist of the original settlement. Thatched-roofed buildings and the Indian Village are all replicas of the originals, as are the three ships lying at anchor in the bay. These few remains, however, are a testimony to the courage and perseverance of our first settlers, who are often overlooked in accounts of the history of our country's beginnings. The settlers at Jamestown did not, like those who would eventually found the Massachusetts Bay Colony, have a vision of themselves as saviors of a civilization or founders of a new and better world. They crossed the Atlantic seeking to establish a profit-making venture; but in so doing they had a profound influence on the future of America, for while they sought merely profit, they found instead the beginnings of a great democracy.

MAN WORKING WITH SKINS
Festival Park, Jamestown, Virginia
E. Carle/Superstock

The Landing of the Pilgrims

William Bradford

Being thus arrived and brought safe to land, they fell upon their knees and blessed the God of heaven who had brought them over the vast and furious ocean, and delivered them from all the perils and miseries thereof, again to set their feet on the firm and stable earth . . . Being thus past the vast ocean, and a sea of troubles before in their preparation, they had now no friends to welcome them, no inns to entertain or refresh their weather-beaten bodies, no houses or much less towns to repair to, to seek for succor. It is recorded in Scripture as a mercy to the apostle and his ship-wrecked company that the barbarians showed them no small kindness in refreshing them; but these savage barbarians, when they met with them, were readier to fill their sides full of arrows . . . And for the season, it was winter, and they that know the winters of that country know them to be sharp and violent and subject to cruel and fierce storms, dangerous to travel to known places, much more to search an unknown coast.

Besides, what could they see but a hideous and desolate wilderness, full of wild beasts and wild men? and what multitudes of them there might be they knew not . . . Which way so ever they turned their eyes (save upwards to the heavens) they could have little solace or content in respect of any outward objects. For summer being done, all things stand upon them with a weather-beaten face; and the whole country, full of woods and thickets, represented a savage and wild hue. If they looked behind them, there was the mighty ocean they had passed and was now as a main bar and gulf to separate them from all the civil parts of the world. . .

What could sustain them but the spirit of God and his grace? May not and ought not the children of these fathers rightly say: "Our fathers were Englishmen which came over this great ocean and were ready to perish in the wilderness; but they cried unto the Lord, and he heard their voices and looked on their adversity. Let them therefore praise the Lord because he is good and his mercies endure forever . . ."

Art by Russ Flint

The First Thanksgiving of All

Nancy Byrd Turner

Peace and Mercy and Jonathan,
And Patience (very small),
Stood by the table giving thanks
The first Thanksgiving of all.
There was very little for them to eat,
Nothing special and nothing sweet;
Only bread and a little broth,
And a bit of fruit (and no tablecoth);
But Peace and Mercy and Jonathan
And Patience in a row,
Stood up and asked a blessing on
Thanksgiving, long ago.
Thankful they were their ship had come
Safely across the sea;
Thankful they were for hearth and home,
And kin and company;
They were glad of broth to go with their bread,
Glad their apples were round and red,
Glad of mayflowers they would bring
Out of the woods again next spring.

COLLECTOR'S CORNER

Political Memorabilia

Carol Shaw Johnston

The American political arena of the past and present provides vast resources for the collector. During George Washington's time and the years immediately following, political materials were mostly for the commemoration of events. However, the political scene changed in the 1830s with the advent of the two-party system, which made it necessary for candidates to seek support directly from their constituents. Over the years a wide variety of objects was produced to promote these campaigns.

Collectors of political memorabilia have divided presidential campaign history into eras. Each era is marked by characteristic trends or issues. The first was the Era of the Founding Fathers, from 1789 to 1830. This was an era of very dignified campaigning; our first five presidents were all active in seeking American independence from Great Britain, but at that time candidates never actively sought votes from the public. For this reason collectors look for commemorative pieces rather than campaign artifacts. George Washington inaugural buttons are the top choice items from this era.

The second era in American political memorabilia collecting is that of the Common Man. This lasted from 1830 until the presidency of Abraham Lincoln. Andrew Jackson defined this era with his humble beginnings and his "common man" lifestyle; Jackson was a candidate with whom most voters could identify, and today, he is a figure with a great deal of appeal to collectors.

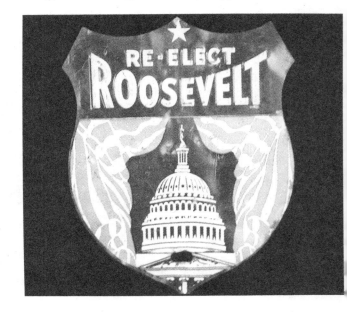

Artifacts from this era include a brass log cabin button from the 1840 campaign, which was the first American political campaign button. This year also brought the first campaign parades and rallies and the first slogan—"Tippecanoe and Tyler too!"

The next era in political campaign collecting is that of Abraham Lincoln. Lincoln collectibles tend to be more expensive than those from other presidencies, simply because he ranks as one of the outstanding characters in American history. After the Lincoln era came the Boom and Bust period of 1872-1892. During this time there was a power shift from rural areas to cities, from farms to factories. Campaign material from these years was printed in more than a dozen languages in order to appeal to the large numbers of potential voters among recent immigrants from southern and central Europe. Following this was the Gold, Silver, and Internationalism era of 1896-1916, highlighted by the race between William Jennings Bryan and William McKinley in 1896. Later, Teddy Roosevelt, with his aggressive personality, and William Howard Taft, with his rotund figure, provided an abundance of material for collectors.

The years between 1920 and 1945 are referred to as the Era of Normalcy, Depression, and the New Deal. Democratic material from these years is very scarce, thus quite valuable. Warren G. Harding, Calvin Coolidge, James M. Cox, Franklin Delano Roosevelt, John Davis, Charles Bryan, Al Smith, Herbert Hoover, Wendell Wilkie, and Thomas Dewey were all prominent political figures of this era, and each produced campaign material now valued by collectors.

Today, we live in the Jet Age of political campaigning. Since 1948, campaigns have been defined by television and jet travel. Campaigning is now big business and campaign materials exist in great abundance. With such availability, collectors tend to concentrate on the truly remarkable political figures, people like John F. Kennedy, who have become icons of American history.

Many people think of political items simply as campaign buttons. There is, however, an abundance of other material related to campaigns —newspapers, pamphlets, glassware, textiles, and various novelty items. Some collectors concentrate on a particular era; others devote them-

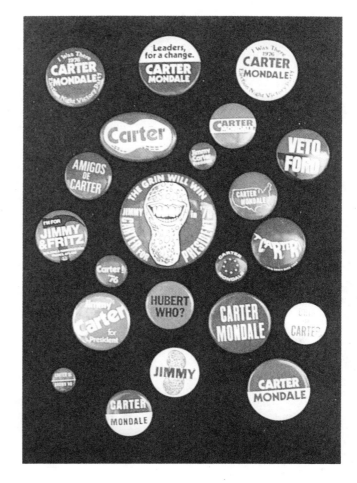

selves to an individual, including in their collections books, photos, and anything they find relating to their era or their candidate.

Regardless of the era or specialization, collecting political memorabilia is a fascinating pastime, and it is also a wonderful way to learn about and celebrate America's unique history.

Thanksgiving Prayer

Angela Gall

Father I thank Thee most for faith—
A faith that blossoms in the snow
And has the will of timber lines
That weave and bend as fierce winds blow;
A faith that knows a season's turn,
Somehow, will see the cold, hard sod
Mellow and warm beneath the plow.
Thank Thee for saving faith, my God.

Photo Opposite
AUTUMN GLADE
Bridgewater, Vermont
enry J. Hupp/Laatsch-Hupp Photo

THROUGH MY WINDOW
Pamela Kennedy

R.FLINT

A Gratitude Attitude

Thanksgiving is on the way and cornucopias are spilling their abundant contents on greeting cards and paper tablecloths, honeycomb centerpieces, and party invitations. The stores are filled with plump turkeys and portly pumpkins destined for family feasts. We become obsessed with thankfulness this time of year, as if making up for months spent in selfish indulgence.

Of course, ironically, it is indulgence which most marks this festival of thanks we celebrate each November. Now is the time for remembering the gifts we enjoy—treasures of friends and family, health and home. These are the common and obvious blessings; but there are others, more subtle, yet just as real that, appreciated, make Thanksgiving not only an annual celebration, but a philosophy—a gratitude attitude.

Each day, indeed each hour, of life is so filled with the wonder of discovery that it seems a shame so many stumble through life depressed and discouraged. Perhaps if we were to fine-tune our focus so as to view more clearly the smaller joys life gives we would find Thanksgiving creeping into every day.

Who has not known the wonder and joy of stumbling upon a spider's web, embroidered with the morning dew? Or caught the pulsing rainbow of a butterfly resting in the sun? A stone polished by the tumbling surf or a bubbling brook brings delight with both its color and texture. The intricate weaving of a swallow's nest or the brilliant blue of a robin's egg causes us to wonder at a creator who brings not only order, but beauty to the natural world. And when we see these natural phenomena, shouldn't gratitude fill our hearts that we, too, are part of this?

The perfection of organic balance that knits bone and blood together in a symphony of life and motion should send us to our knees in thanks. Who among us can add one heartbeat to his life by will or reasoned argument, yet moment by moment, day after day, waking and sleeping, our lives continue in the rhythm set in motion long before our birth. What a gift is life! How grateful we should be for the span we are allotted!

If we, as adults, have lost the ability to find cause for gratitude in the everyday, we would do well to take a child by the hand and wander for an hour or two.

"Oh, Mama, look at the cottonwood seeds in the wind! Doesn't it look like it's snowing?"

"See the stripe on the garter snake's back? Watch how he slides through the grass!"

"Smell the sea, Grandma? Doesn't it make you want to sail far away?"

No, there's nothing like a child to remind us to be thankful for the little things in life.

But then, there are other things that can only be truly appreciated by those of us who have traveled far past childhood. It takes a bit of living to be overwhelmed with gratitude at the hand of a friend extended at a moment of grief. There are times when a gentle hug, a warm smile, a pat on the back, or a squeeze on the arm fill us with thanks as well. The little gestures of understanding which bind us to others give us courage to continue. If we not only look for them, but seek opportunities to offer them, we cultivate an attitude of gratitude that enriches the quality of life.

Long after the Thanksgiving prayers are over, when the turkey and dressing have made their last contribution to the leftover menu, winter days will stretch before us. We can look back longingly to the warmth of the Festival Day of Thanks, or forward to a year of thankfulness. May your coming months be marked by the blessing of a gratitude attitude for life's simplest gifts, offered in the humble wrapping of ordinary days.

Pamela Kennedy is a freelance writer of short stories, articles, essays, and children's books. Married to a naval officer and mother of three children, she has made her home on both U.S. coasts and currently resides in Hawaii. She draws her material from her own experiences and memories, adding bits of imagination to create a story or mood.

Service

Alice B. Dorland

Let us count service
As the deepest of our joys.
It is the salt and savor
Of our every day.

'Tis that by which
The heart is warmed,
Our antidote for loneliness,
Our balm in Gilead.

Service asks no recompense,
It is its own reward.
But, like bread cast upon the waters,
It will return to us
In its own time,
In its own way.

COUNTRY CHURCH IN AUTUMN
Hillsboro Center, New Hampshire
Dick Smith, Photographer

For Everything Give Thanks

Helena Isabella Tupper

For all that God in mercy sends,
For health and children, home and friends,
For comfort in the time of need,
For every kindly word and deed,
For happy thoughts and holy talk,
For guidance in our daily walk,
    For everything give thanks!

For beauty in this world of ours,
For verdant grass and lovely flowers,
For song of bird, for hum of bees,
For refreshing summer breeze,
For hill and plain, for streams and wood,
For the great ocean's mighty flood,
    For everything give thanks!

For sweet sleep which comes with night,
For the returning morning light,
For the bright sun that shines on high,
For the stars glittering in the sky,
For these and everything we see,
O Lord, our hearts we lift to thee.
    For everything give thanks!

Our Own Thanksgiving Day

Mary R. Ellis

We thank Thee, Lord,
   and render praise
For many gifts and length of days;
For benefits and joys apace,
For happiness and Thy good grace,
For friends and kindred
   and for home
That we, like many, need not roam
Afar in alien lands. We greet
With thankful hearts our Lord.
   We meet
In reverent communion sweet,
To bow before the mercy seat.
All that we are or have we bring
With thankful hearts to our great king.
We praise and thank,
   rejoice and pray
On this our own Thanksgiving Day.

OLD SHIPS AT MYSTIC SEAPORT
Mystic, Connecticut
William Johnson, Photographer

The Oak Leaves

Edna St. Vincent Millay

Yet in the end, defeated too, worn out and ready to fall,
Hangs from the drowsy tree with cramped and desperate
stem above the ditch the last leaf of all.

There is something to be learned, I guess, from looking at
the dead leaves under the living tree;
Something to be set to a lusty tune and learned and sung,
it well might be;

Something to be learned—though I was ever a
    ten-o'clock scholar at this school—
Even perhaps by me.

But my heart goes out to the oak-leaves that are
    the last to sigh
"Enough," and loose their hold;
They have boasted to the nudging frost and to the two-
    and-thirty winds that they would never die,
Never even grow old.
(These are those russet leaves that cling all winter, even
    into the spring,
To the dormant bough, in the wood
    knee-deep in the snow the only coloured thing.)

Let Autumn Linger

May Smith White

Why cannot the beauty
    of this Autumn last?
Each leaf falls, now blends
    with browning earth,
But all too soon this beauty will be past,
And we, like buds, must wait the
    new Spring's birth.
While leaves turn back to soil
    that gave them strength,
Forsaken birds' nests sway alone and bare;
And as we near the season's
    waning length
This quiet time is all mankind's to share.

May each of us be somewhat
    like the leaves:
They give their all, yet are
    not discontent.
Let each rejoice for that
    which he receives,
Recalling now the quiet Autumn lent.
Like greening leaves
    encountering the frost
May we regret no earlier beauty lost.

HORSE AND CARRIAGE
Lancaster County, Pennsylvania
J. Irwin/H. Armstrong Roberts, Inc.

The Rainy Day

Henry Wadsworth Longfellow

The day is cold, and dark, and dreary,
It rains, and the wind is never weary;
The vine still clings to the mouldering wall,
But at every gust the dead leaves fall,
   And the day is dark and dreary.

My life is cold, and dark, and dreary;
It rains, and the wind is never weary;
My thoughts still cling to the mouldering Past,
But the hopes of youth fall thick in the blast,
   And the days are dark and dreary.

Be still, sad heart; and cease repining;
Behind the clouds is the sun still shining;
Thy fate is the common fate of all,
Into each life some rain must fall,
   Some days must be dark and dreary.

The Constancy of Seasons

May Smith White

Each falling leaf today is autumn-wise.
    A deep conspiracy is close at hand,
    As leaves all move like some great rhythmic band
    And, from the distance, come the wild-geese cries.

Each season seems a mystery that lies
    As if deep-buried in the quiet land;
    And many times in awe we mutely stand
    Because it always leaves some broken ties.

We grow complacent in these present times
    And fail to plan for days that lie ahead—
    Like nature plans for changes sure to come
    As suddenly as do a poet's rhymes.

We must be like the seasons—hold no dread,
    But harvest now each final autumn crumb.

Photo Opposite
WINTER SURPRISES AUTUMN
Lititz, Pennsylvania
arry Lefever/Grant Heilman Photography, Inc.

BITS & PIECES

O come, let us sing unto the Lord: let us heartily rejoice in the strength of our salvation. Let us come before his presence with thanksgiving and show ourselves glad in Him with psalms.

The Book of Common Prayer

One single grateful thought raised to heaven is the most perfect prayer.

G. E. Lessing

The best thing to give to your enemy is forgiveness; to an opponent, tolerance; to a friend, your heart; to your child, a good example; to a father, deference; to your mother, conduct that will make her proud of you; to yourself, respect; to all men, charity.

Francis Balfour

Give what you have. To someone it may be better than you dare to think.

Henry Wadsworth Longfellow

O give thanks unto the Lord, for he is good: for his mercy endureth forever.

Psalms 107:1

God has two dwellings: one in heaven and the other in a meek and thankful heart.

Izaak Walton

The worship most acceptable to God comes from a thankful and cheerful heart.

Plutarch

The heart of the giver makes the gift rare and precious.

Martin Luther

When a friend asks, there is no tomorrow.

George Herbert

The private and personal blessing we enjoy, the blessings of immunity, safeguard, liberty and integrity, deserve the thanksgiving of a whole life.

Jeremy Taylor

Behold, I do not give lectures or a little charity. When I give I give myself.

Walt Whitman

You give but little when you give of your possessions. It is when you give of yourself that you truly give.

Kahlil Gibran

We should give as we would receive: cheerfully, quickly, and without hesitation; for there is no grace in a benefit that sticks to the fingers.

Seneca

He Who Waits at Twilight

Lillian Crane Hunter

Did you ever sit at twilight
By your fireside's warm glow,
And try to count your blessings?
It's an endless task, and so
You just breathe a prayer
    of thankfulness,
And sit with half-crossed eyes,
And listen to the rain outside,
And the wind that blows and sighs.

You are waiting for familiar steps,
And voices at the door.
The baby builds his magic roads of
Blocks upon the floor.
The evening meal is family hour,
The happiest of the day,
And he who waits at twilight
Is blessed beyond repay.

AUTUMN LANDSCAPE
Jenne Farm, Vermont
M. Thonig/H. Armstrong Roberts, Inc.

AUTUMN'S TWILIGHT

Garnet Ann Schultz

As I walk through the twilight of autumn,
The hush of the evening so dim,
I walk in a world full of wonders,
The wonders created by Him,
The night is a mantle of quiet,
My heart is at peace as I go,
And autumn is smiling about me
With beauties my mind treasures so.

There's joy in the twilight of autumn,
In the colors of beauty about,
The reds and the golds shining brightly—
God's wondrous world, without doubt.
The rain is but silver from heaven
With leaves mounting high on the ground,
And good Mother Nature doth sparkle
So quiet—you hear not a sound.

I marvel at twilight in autumn
As the sun slowly fades in the West,
It matches the leaves' glowing colors,
'Tis truly the dearest and best,
God's world is a world ever lovely
With the wonders that nature imparts,
As I walk through the quiet of evening
Autumn's twilight brings peace to my heart.

Thanksgiving Day

Peter Marshall

Lord, Thou hast indeed been bountiful. As we look back over the years, how gracious Thou hast been, how tender Thy mercy, how warm and constant Thy love.

Create within us, our Father, that true gratitude that shall make this day of Thanksgiving one of rededication, when we shall think not of how much we can eat but of how thankful we ought to be.

So may we—all across this land today—act as recipients of God's richest mercy and bountiful blessing, as we share with others. May we, in gratitude, get on with the job of creating not only a nation but a world in which all men shall have the right to seek happiness.

Help us to make that dream come true in our homes day by day, in street and office and school, and so live that Thou shalt be able to bless us and bless this nation for which we pray. In His name, who created us a nation, we pray. Amen.

Photo Opposite
THANKSGIVING PREPARATIONS
Jessie Walker/Jessie Walker Associate

Good-Bye and Keep Cold

Robert Frost

This saying good-bye on the edge of the dark
And the cold to an orchard so young in the bark
Reminds me of all that can happen to harm
An orchard away at the end of the farm
All winter, cut off by a hill from the house.
I don't want it girdled by rabbit and mouse,
I don't want it dreamily nibbled for browse
By deer, and I don't want it budded by grouse.
(If certain it wouldn't be idle to call
I'd summon grouse, rabbit, and deer to the wall
And warn them away with a stick for a gun.)
I don't want it stirred by the heat of the sun.

(We made it secure against being, I hope,
By setting it out on a northerly slope.)
No orchard's the worse for the wintriest storm;
But one thing about it, it mustn't get warm.
'How often already you've had to be told,
Keep cold, young orchard. Good-bye and keep cold.
Dread fifty above more than fifty below.'
I have to be gone for a season or so.
My business awhile is with different trees,
Less carefully nurtured, less fruitful than these,
And such as is done to their wood with an axe—
Maples and birches and tamaracks.
I wish I could promise to lie in the night
And think of an orchard's arboreal plight
When slowly (and nobody comes with a light)
Its heart sinks lower under the sod.
But something has to be left to God.

Readers' Forum

It is with pleasure that I received notice from your magazine to subscribe this date. I returned the card with the gold stamp requesting a free issue.

Picture a 1940s atmosphere, overstuffed furniture, Roseville pottery and Wedgewood china scattered about; simmering potpourri (let's say cinnamon scent) bubbling on the stove in the kitchen and you have a description of my house. I'm 43 going on 44 and on most weekends you'll find me driving my dream car (a 1951 Buick Roadmaster) to an antique store or flea market, digging around for things out of the past. (I have on occasion, seen old copies of Ideals *and often wondered if it was still published!) I like things American and comfortable and your magazine will be a nice addition to my living room.*

I look forward to receiving your magazine, and thanks again for inviting me to subscribe.

Steve Halbrook
Denver, Colorado

Thank you for the very unique and beautiful volumes of Ideals. *I've read them for years from the library but finally decided I had to have them to call my own because I enjoy them so much. They seem to soothe my troubles away and also make my days a little brighter.*

Reba M. Moss
Buffalo, Missouri

My forty-year-old granddaughter gave me a copy of your Mother's Day Ideals *and a note that said:*

"I saw this book in a bookstore and I just had to send it to you for Mother's Day because it brought back so many wonderful memories of looking at all the Ideals *books. I thought they were the prettiest books I had ever seen as a child. It still looks like a pretty neat book. Just couldn't resist. Love you so, Doren."*

I had forgotten Ideals. *In going back in memory, I was looking at my grandmother's hand painted platter—beautiful roses—that hangs on my wall and was in her dining room . . . I was back there. . . . Thank you, and Doren, for taking me back to 1914. In these times, it is so precious to find we haven't lost all the lovely things.*

Gracey Owen
Los Angeles, California

Editor's Note: Readers are invited to submit unpublished, original poetry, short anecdotes, and humorous reflections on life for possible publication in future *Ideals* issues. Please send copies only; manuscripts will not be returned. Writers receive $10 for each published submission. Send material to: "Readers' Reflections," Ideals Publishing Corporation, P.O. Box 140300, Nashville, TN 37214-0300.

Give
ideals® This Christmas!

This year, give a subscription to *ideals*® — the one gift that will express your thoughtfulness many times throughout the coming year.

To order, simply call toll-free at 1-800-558-4343 or complete and return one of the postcards at the right. You may add more gifts at only $19.95 each by enclosing a separate list with additional names and addresses in an envelope and return to: Ideals Publishing Corp., P.O. Box 148000, Nashville, TN 37214, or by calling the number above. You need send no money now, we'll gladly bill you later.

We'll send a greeting card announcing your gift. Subscription will start with *ideals*® Christmas issue. (Orders received after Dec. 5 will start with Valentine issue.)

1-year Gift — only $19.95

Save $19.65 off the bookstore price

Order Now!

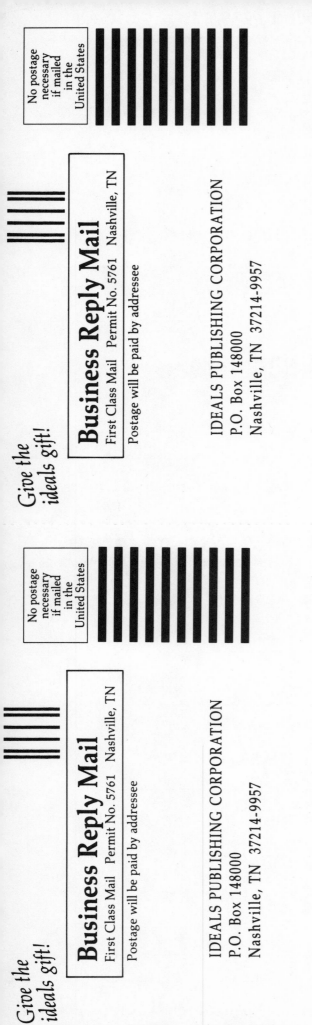

Make Someone Happy

Delight all the special people on your list. Give them *ideals* gift subscriptions.

ideals — the magazine that celebrates life's most treasured moments makes the ideal gift for friends, relatives and business associates.

They'll love it because each issue is filled with beautiful photographs and drawings, heart-warming stories and poems. And *ideals* comes eight times during the year, reminding your friends just how much you care.

Just complete the order side of these cards and mail or telephone your order TOLL FREE. We'll announce your gifts with greeting cards.

Order Today!

Great gardening tips on growing squash pgs. 18-19

Publisher, Patricia A. Pingry
Editor, Nancy J. Skarmeas
Associate Editor, D. Fran Morley
Art Director, Patrick McRae
Contributing Editors, Marty Sowder Brooks, Lansing Christman, Deana Deck, Russ Flint, Carol Shaw Johnston, Pamela Kennedy
Editorial Assistant, LaNita Kirby

ISBN 0-8249-1094-X

IDEALS—Vol. 48, No. 7 November MCMXCI IDEALS (ISSN 0019-137X) is published eight times a year: February, March, May, June, August, September, November, December by IDEALS PUBLISHING CORPORATION, P.O. Box 148000, Nashville, Tenn. 37214. Second-class postage paid at Nashville, Tennessee, and additional mailing offices. Copyright © MCMXCI by IDEALS PUBLISHING CORPORATION. POSTMASTER: Send address changes to Ideals, Post Office Box 148000, Nashville, Tenn. 37214-8000. All rights reserved. Title IDEALS registered U.S. Patent Office.

SINGLE ISSUE—$4.95
ONE-YEAR SUBSCRIPTION—eight consecutive issues as published—$19.95
TWO-YEAR SUBSCRIPTION—sixteen consecutive issues as published—$35.95
Outside U.S.A., add $6.00 per subscription year for postage and handling.

GOOD-BY AND KEEP COLD by Robert Frost. From *THE POETRY OF ROBERT FROST* edited by Edward Connery Lathem. Copyright 1923, © 1969 by Holt, Rinehart and Winston. Copyright 1951 by Robert Frost. Reprinted by permission of Henry Holt and Company, Inc.; THANKSGIVING PRAYER from *THROUGH TINTED PANES*. © 1964 by Angela Gall; THANKSGIVING from *A HEAP O' LIVIN'* by Edgar A. Guest. © 1916 by The Reilly & Britton Co.: Used by permission of the estate; THANKSGIVING DAY from *THE PRAYERS OF PETER MARSHALL*, edited by Catherine Marshall copyright © 1949, 1950, 1951, 1954 by Catherine Marshall. Renewed 1982. Published by Chosen Books, Fleming H. Revell Company. Used by permission; KEY TO JOY by Lucile V. McCurtain. From *BEST LOVED UNITY POEMS*, published by Unity School of Christianity in 1956: Used by permission of the estate; THE OAK-LEAVES by Edna St. Vincent Millay. From *COLLECTED POEMS*, Harper & Row. Copyright © 1934, 1962 by Edna St. Vincent Millay and Norma Millay Ellis. Reprinted by permission of Elizabeth Barnett, literary executor; FIRST THANKSGIVING from *THE SHINING THREAD* by Jessie Wilmore Murton. © Pacific Press Publishing Association. Used by permission; AUTUMN'S TWILIGHT from book *MOMENTS OF SUNSHINE*. Copyrighted—Used by permission of author; NOVEMBER from *THE STILLMEADOW ROAD* by Gladys Taber Copyright © 1959, 1960, 1962, by Gladys Taber Copyright renewed © 1990 by Constance Taber Colby. Reprinted by permission of Brandt & Brandt Literary Agents, Inc.; FIRST THANKSGIVING OF ALL by Nancy Byrd Turner: Used by permission of Beverley T. Thomas. Our sincere thanks to the following whose addresses we were unable to locate: The estate of Alice B. Dorland for the poems BEAUTY and SERVICE from *ROAMING THE WIND*. © 1955 by Alice B. Dorland; Mary R. Ellis for OUR OWN THANKSGIVING DAY. Published under the title THANKSGIVING in *ANTHOLOGY OF NEWSPAPER VERSE*. © 1924 by Franklyn Pierre Davis; Lillian Crane Hunter for HE WHO WAITS AT TWILIGHT from *HOMESPUN*. Copyright 1936 by American Book Company; Lillian C. Parkin for GATEWAY TO HEAVEN; Estelle S. Rizk for THANKSGIVING from *TO A TIMBERLINE TREE*; Gloria Ingram Roberts for THANKSGIVING SEASON. Published as THANKSGIVING in *IN WHITE STARLIGHT*. © 1962 by Gloria Ingram; Helena Isabella Tupper for FOR EVERYTHING GIVE THANKS; May Smith White for LET AUTUMN LINGER; May Smith White for THE CONSTANCY OF SEASONS from *FORTY ACRES*. © 1949 by May Smith White.

Unsolicited manuscripts will not be returned without a self-addressed stamped envelope.

Four-color separations by Rayson Films, Inc., Waukesha, Wisconsin

Printing by The Banta Company, Menasha, Wisconsin

Inside Front Cover
VISITING PILGRIMS
John Walter

Inside Back Cover
OLD FOLKS
George Hinke

Cover Photo
TOWN COMMON AND MEETING HOUSE
Jaffrey Center, New Hampshire
H. Abernathy/H. Armstrong Roberts

Vol. 48, No. 7

November

Gladys Taber

Now in November, the leaves spread cloth of gold and red on the ground. The open fields take on a cinnamon tone and the wild blackberry canes in the swamp are frosted purple. The colors fade slowly to sober hues. The rain falls with a determination in long leaden lines, and when it stops water drips from the eaves.

The voice of the wind changes, for the winds are seasonal too. Summer winds blow soft, musical with leaves, except for thunderstorms. Hurricane winds scream. In blizzard time the sleet-sharp gale has a crackling noise. But now the wind has a mournful sound, marking the rhythm of autumn's end. The first beat of winter is not yet here, and country folks tend to spend extra time doing chores or puttering, just to be out of doors.

When Indian summer comes, nothing indoors seems important. I must carry my breakfast tray to the terrace and eat in the wine-bright sun. There is always a haze on the hills, making them dream-like. Eternal summer shines from a soft sky. Perhaps it is such an enchanted time because it is a promise that another summer will come, after winter goes. Actually, there is no set date for Indian summer, it comes when it is ready. Sometimes it seems to come after a cold spell in October, but it may even come around Thanksgiving. The later it comes the better, I think, like an extra dividend.

Usually it ends with a swift drop in temperature and grey skies. Frost whitens the lawn and too soon snow-lace drops on the bushes. We proceed with November.

Photo Opposite
BLOODBROOK ROAD
Near Lake Fairlee, Vermont
Grant Heilman/Grant Heilman Photography,